Easy Learning

English

Age 4-5

My name is ....

I am .... years old.

My favourite book is ....

Illustrated by Rachel Annie Bridgen

How to use this book

- Find a quiet, comfortable place to work, away from other distractions.

- Tackle one topic at a time.

- Help with reading the instructions where necessary, and ensure that your child understands what to do.

- Discuss with your child what they have learnt.

- Let your child return to their favourite pages once they have been completed, to talk about the activities.

- Reward your child with plenty of praise and encouragement.

- Please note that some schools use different handwriting styles to this book. Check which style your child's school uses.

Special features

- Parent's notes: These are divided into 'What you need to know', which explain the key English idea, and 'Taking it further', which suggest activities and encourage discussion with your child about what they have learnt. The words in bold are key words that you should focus on when talking to your child.

Published by Collins
An imprint of HarperCollins*Publishers*
77–85 Fulham Palace Road
Hammersmith
London
W6 8JB

Browse the complete Collins catalogue at
www.collins.co.uk

First published in 2006
© HarperCollins*Publishers* 2008

10 9 8

ISBN-13 978-0-00-730104-1

British Library Cataloguing in Publication Data
A Catalogue record for this publication is available from the British Library

Design and layout by Lodestone Publishing Limited, Uckfield, East Sussex; www.lodestonepublishing.com
Illustrated by Rachel Annie Bridgen;
www.shootingthelight.com
Handwriting artwork by Kathy Baxendale
Cover design by Susi Martin
Cover illustration by John Haslam
Printed and bound China

Contents

- Trace.

- Say **c** in

  Find **c** in   **c**at   **c**ow   **c**up

  Write.

  _____

- Say **o** in

  Find **o** in   **o**ff   **o**range   **o**ctopus

  Write.

  _____

- Say **a** in

  Find **a** in   **a**nt   **a**pple   **a**mbulance

  Write.

  _____

What you need to know   The letters of the alphabet are introduced by shape, the first group being round letters, and the second straight letters. Encourage your child to start with the sound, first saying the sound of 'c...' as in 'cat', not the letter **c**. Then to recognise the shape of the letter (trace it with a finger, write it in the air together, and finally try writing it).

Letters i, l, t

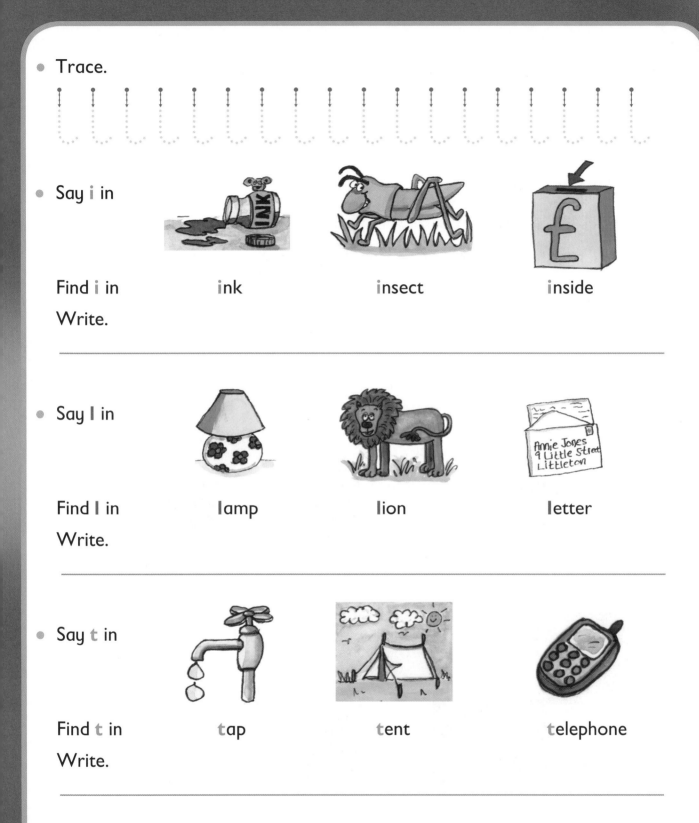

- Trace.

- Say i in

  Find i in   ink   insect   inside
  Write.

- Say l in

  Find l in   lamp   lion   letter
  Write.

- Say t in

  Find t in   tap   tent   telephone
  Write.

Taking it further   Play I Spy with words beginning with the alphabet sounds. Look out for the letters on packets of food. (Keep to the short vowel sounds, e.g. ant, egg, ink, orange, umbrella, and avoid the long vowel sounds, as in alien, easy, ice cream, uniform.) Do more writing practice together – the size of the letters is not important at this stage.

- Trace.

- Say **r** in

Find **r** in   **r**un   **r**abbit   **r**ing
Write.

_____

- Say **n** in

Find **n** in   **n**et   **n**ut   **n**est
Write.

_____

- Say **m** in

Find **m** in   **m**oon   **m**oney   **m**ouse
Write.

_____

- Trace.

- Say **u** in

  Find **u** in   **u**p   **u**nder   **u**mbrella
  Write.

_____

- Say **y** in

  Find **y** in   **y**ellow   **y**oyo   **y**olk
  Write.

_____

- Say **j** in

  Find **j** in   **j**am   **j**ug   **j**elly
  Write.

_____

● Trace.

ccccccccar

● Say **d** in

Find **d** in   **d**og   **d**ish   **d**uck

Write.

_____

● Say **g** in

Find **g** in   **g**irl   **g**ate   **g**host

Write.

_____

● Say **q** in

Find **q** in   **q**ueen   **q**uestion   **q**uick

Write.

_____

Letters f, s, e

- Trace.

- Say **f** in

Find **f** in   **f**ish   **f**eather   **f**inger
Write.

_____

- Say **s** in

Find **s** in   **s**un   **s**ix   **s**nake
Write.

_____

- Say **e** in

Find **e** in   **e**gg   **e**lephant   **e**nvelope
Write.

_____

Letters h, k, b, p

Trace. h h k k b b p p

Say **h** in

Find **h** in   **h**at   **h**en   **h**ouse

Write.

Say **k** in

Find **k** in   **k**ing   **k**ite   **k**ey

Write.

Say **b** in

Find **b** in   **b**ed   **b**at   **b**all

Write.

Say **p** in

Find **p** in   **p**in   **p**ath   **p**enguin

Write.

Letters v, w, x, z

- Trace.

- Say **v** in

  Find **v** in   **v**ase   **v**iolin   **v**ulture
  Write.

  _____

- Say **w** in

  Find **w** in   **w**eb   **w**ave   **w**indow
  Write.

  _____

- Say **x** in

  Find **x** in   fo**x**   si**x**   wa**x**
  Write.

  _____

- Say **z** in

  Find **z** in   **z**ebra   **zzz**
  Write.

  _____

Alphabetical order

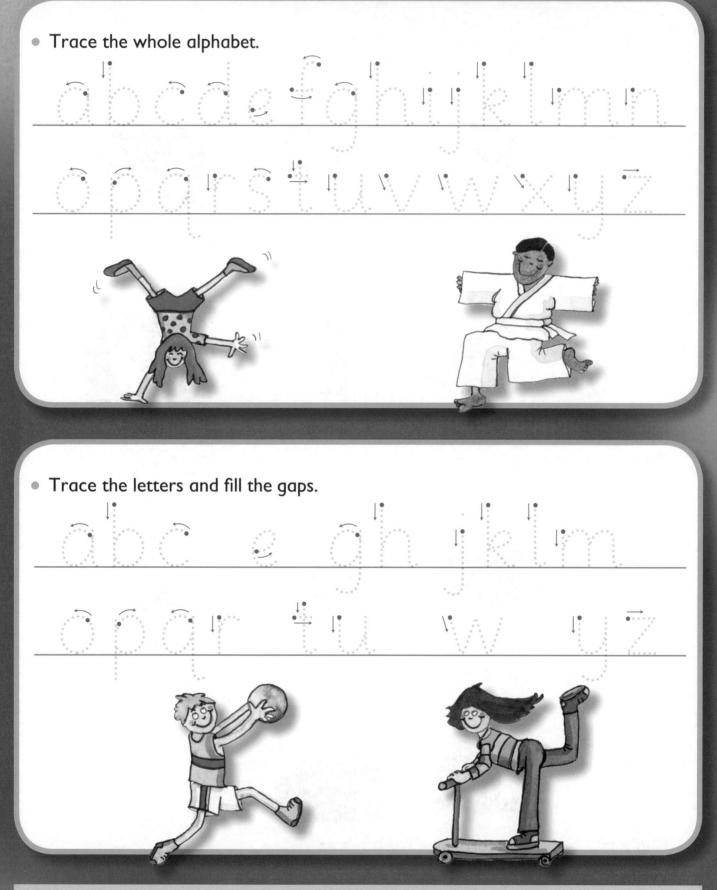

- Trace the whole alphabet.

abcdefghijklmn
opqrstuvwxyz

- Trace the letters and fill the gaps.

abc e gh jklm
opqr tu w uz

What you need to know   Having introduced the letters by shape, it is time to put them together in alphabetical order. Talk with your child about how useful alphabetical order is and how it helps us when we use phone books, dictionaries, and libraries.

- Think of a food for each letter of the alphabet.

- Join the dots.

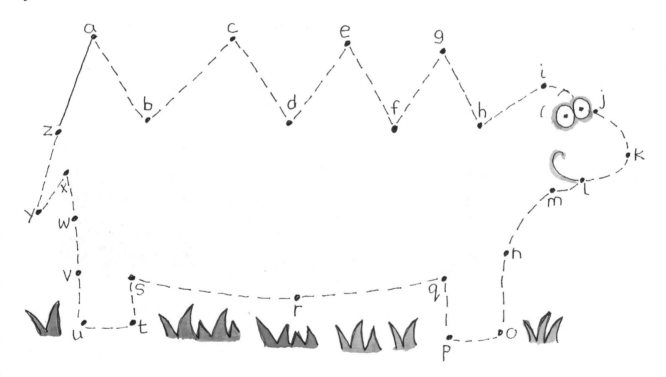

Finish colouring the picture.

ch, sh, th

- Say **sh** in

Find **sh** in   **sh**ip   **sh**eep   fi**sh**

Write.   ___ ___ ip   ___ ___ eep   fi ___ ___

- Say **ch** in

  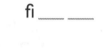

Find **ch** in   **ch**ips   **ch**eese   ri**ch**

Write.   ___ ___ ips   ___ ___ eese   ri ___ ___

- Say **th** in

Find **th** in   **th**in   ba**th**   pa**th**

Write.   ___ ___ in   ba ___ ___   pa ___ ___

What you need to know   The pairs of letters **ch**, **sh**, **th** are pronounced as a single sound, and are common in lots of words.

Build words with a

Fill in the missing letter.

cat

h___ t

m___ t

pan

f___ n

r___ n

c ___ ___

m ___ ___

f ___ ___

r ___ ___

h ___ ___

p ___ ___

Build words with a

Taking it further   Think of more words that rhyme with the lists above: cat, hat, mat, bat, pat, sat, etc.

Build words with e

● Fill in the missing letter.

net   p___t   w___t

hen   p___n   t___n

n___ ___   P ___ ___   h___ ___

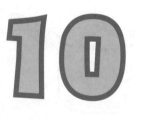

t___ ___   w___ ___   p___ ___

What you need to know These 3-letter words are called CVC (**c**onsonant – **v**owel – **c**onsonant) words. They are the first words that children can begin to build from the individual letters.

● Fill in the missing letter.

pin

f __ n

t __ n

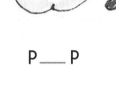

zip

P __ P

l __ p

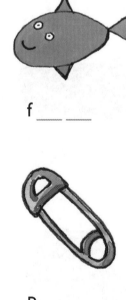

P __ __

l __ __

f __ __

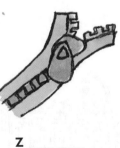

z __ __

t __ __

p __ __

Taking it further   Think of more words that rhyme with the lists above: pin, fin, tin, bin, din, win, etc.

Build words with o

Fill in the missing letter.

dog

l___g

f___g

hot

c___t

p___t

l_____

p_____

f_____

h_____

d_____

c_____

Build words with u

● Fill in the missing letter.

mug

r___g

j___g

sun

b___n

r___n

j_____

b_____

s_____

r_____

m_____

r_____

Taking it further   Think of more words that rhyme with the lists above: mug, rug, jug, bug, hug, tug, etc.

19

Rhymes

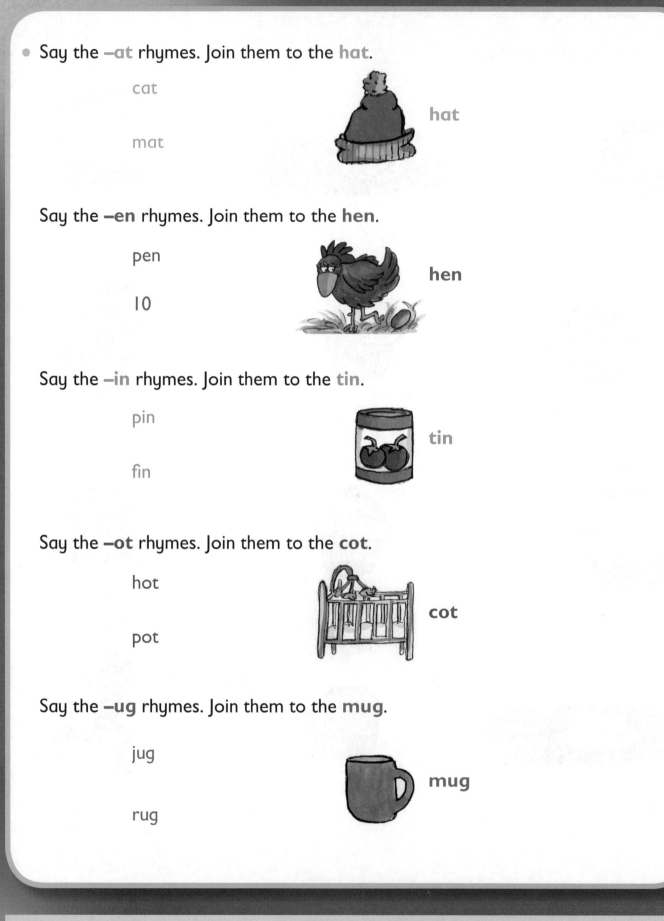

- Say the –at rhymes. Join them to the **hat**.

  cat

  mat

  hat

Say the **–en** rhymes. Join them to the **hen**.

  pen

  10

  hen

Say the **–in** rhymes. Join them to the **tin**.

  pin

  fin

  tin

Say the **–ot** rhymes. Join them to the **cot**.

  hot

  pot

  cot

Say the **–ug** rhymes. Join them to the **mug**.

  jug

  rug

  mug

What you need to know   Rhyming is an important way of recognising the spelling pattern of similar words, e.g. that all the **–at** words are spelt with the same ending.

- Fill the hat with **–at** rhymes.

Fill the hen with **–en** rhymes.

Fill the tin with **–in** rhymes.

Fill the cot with **–ot** rhymes.

Fill the mug with **–ug** rhymes.

Taking it further   Recite nursery rhymes together, emphasising the rhyming words at the end of the lines.

21

Number words

- Sing the rhyme.

One, two, three, four, five
Once I caught a fish alive;
Six, seven, eight, nine, ten
Then I let it go again.

- Match the words to the numbers.

one   two   three   four   five   six   seven   eight   nine   ten

1 2 3 4 5 6 7 8 9 10

What you need to know   Although numbers are introduced in Reception, the words for one to ten are usually introduced in school from Year 1. As they feature in lots of nursery rhymes, it is useful for pre-school children to recognise and copy them.

● Copy the words.

1	2	3	4	5
One	two	three	four	five

——— ——— ——— ——— ———

Once I caught a fish alive;

6	7	8	9	10
Six	seven	eight	nine	ten

——— ——— ——— ——— ———

Then I let it go again.

● Now write these numbers as words.

6	2	10	3

——— ——— ——— ———

Colours and places

- Copy the words. Fill in the colours.

red ＿ ＿ ＿

blue ＿ ＿ ＿ ＿

green ＿ ＿ ＿ ＿ ＿

yellow ＿ ＿ ＿ ＿ ＿ ＿

black ＿ ＿ ＿ ＿ ＿

brown ＿ ＿ ＿ ＿ ＿

pink ＿ ＿ ＿ ＿

orange ＿ ＿ ＿ ＿ ＿ ＿

What you need to know Colours are useful words to recognise and copy. Most of the words about position are listed as high frequency words, and will also help your child's early maths awareness.

Where are they? Use these words.

under   at   up   on   to   behind   in

Jack and Jill went ___ ___ the hill.

Fly ___ ___ the moon.

We are ___ ___ home.

Cat ___ ___ the mat.

Puss ___ ___ boots.

___ ___ ___ ___ ___ the table.

___ ___ ___ ___ ___ ___ the clock.

Capital letters

- Trace and copy the capital letters.

A A · B B · C C · D D · E E

F F · G G · H H · I I · J J

K K · L L · M M · N N · O O

P P · Q Q · R R · S S · T T

U U · V V · W W · X X

Y Y · Z Z

- Join the matching big and small letters.

W

A   f   S

w

s

k   a   F

c

w

G

C   K   P   p

What you need to know   Children should know that capital letters are used for names. They should be able to write their own name, and once they are familiar with all the small letters to write the alphabet in capitals.

We use capital letters for names.

- Copy and say these names.

| Dan | Beth | Kim | Tom | Gus |

—— —— ——   —— —— —— ——   —— —— ——   —— —— —— ——   —— —— ——

Write your name. _____

Write your brother or sister's name. _____

Write your best friend's name. _____

Taking it further   Help your child to write names on birthday cards, invitations and postcards.

27

Days and seasons

There are seven days of the week.

- Copy the days.

Monday _____	**Friday** _____
Tuesday _____	Saturday _____
Wednesday _____	**Sunday** _____
Thursday _____	

What day is it today? _____

What day is it tomorrow? _____

What day was it yesterday? _____

What you need to know   It is useful to recognise and copy the days of the week as they use capital letters and small letters.

- Match the weather.

  What is it like in Winter?

  What is it like in Summer?

  What is it like in Spring?

  What is it like in Autumn?

hot

cold

snowy

windy

rainy

cloudy

- What is the weather today?

  _____

  Draw a picture.

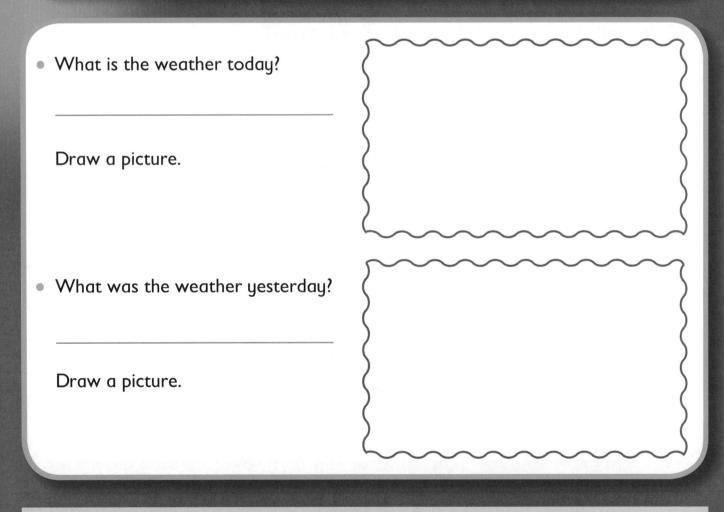

- What was the weather yesterday?

  _____

  Draw a picture.

Taking it further   Make a diary and write down the weather for each day of the week.

- Find words to make sentences.

I	go	come	went	up	you	day	was
look	are	the	of	we	this	dog	me
like	going	big	she	and	they	my	see
on	away	mum	it	at	play	no	yes
for	a	dad	can	he	am	all	
is	cat	get	said	to	in		

I play with my ___ ___ ___ .

I play with ___ ___   ___ ___ ___ .

Mum said ___ ___ ___ .

What you need to know   The words in the table are the 45 high frequency words that children need to be able to read on sight by the end of the Reception year. They don't need to know what a sentence is, but they should be used to hearing how stories, read aloud, make sense using capital letters and full stops.

- Now write your own sentences, using just the words in the box on page 30.

_____

_____

_____

_____

- Draw a picture for one of your sentences.

High frequency words

- Colour each box when you can read and write the word.

I	go	come	went	up	you	day	was
look	are	the	of	we	this	dog	me
like	going	big	she	and	they	my	see
on	away	mum	it	at	play	no	yes
for	a	dad	can	he	am	all	
is	cat	get	said	to	in